Fun & Christmas Songs

Arranged by Dan Coates

Alfred

Santa Claus Is Comin' to Town

Words by
Haven Gillespie

Music by
J. Fred Coots
Arranged by Dan Coates

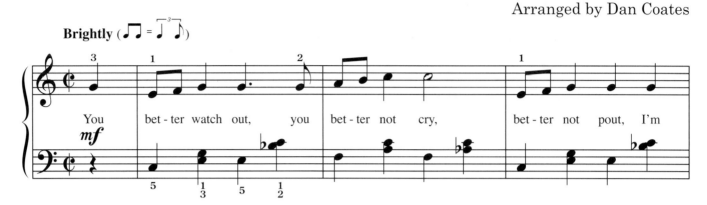

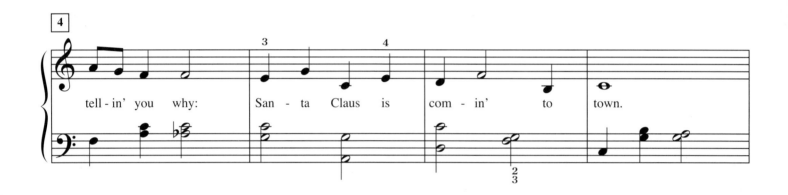

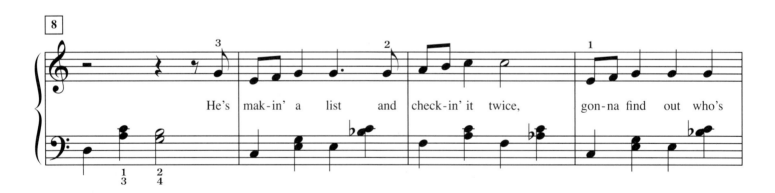

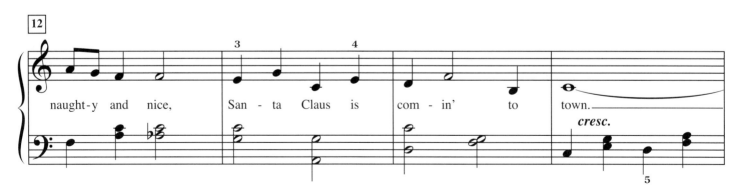

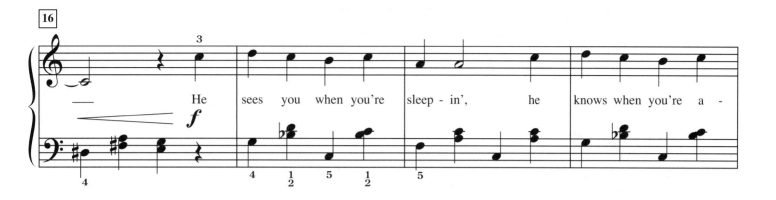

He sees you when you're sleep - in', he knows when you're a -

wake. He knows if you've been bad or good, so be good for good - ness

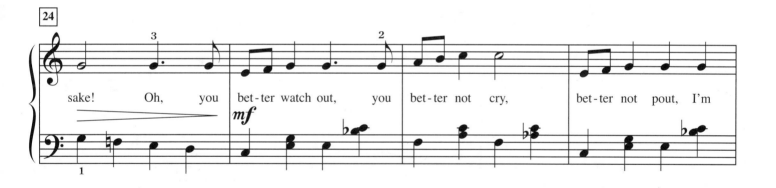

sake! Oh, you bet - ter watch out, you bet - ter not cry, bet - ter not pout, I'm

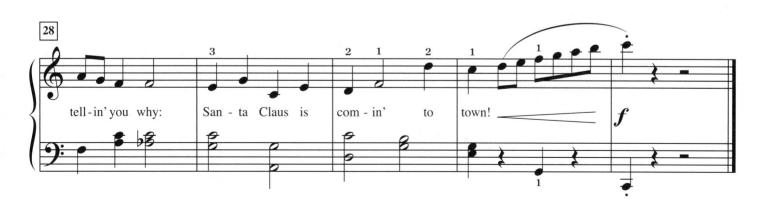

tell - in' you why: San - ta Claus is com - in' to town!

Believe
(From *The Polar Express*)

Words and Music by
Glen Ballard and Alan Silvestri
Arranged by Dan Coates

It's the Most Wonderful Time of the Year

Words and Music by
Eddie Pola and George Wylie
Arranged by Dan Coates

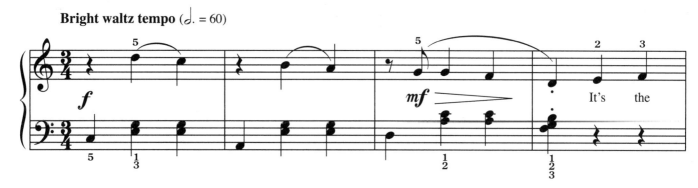

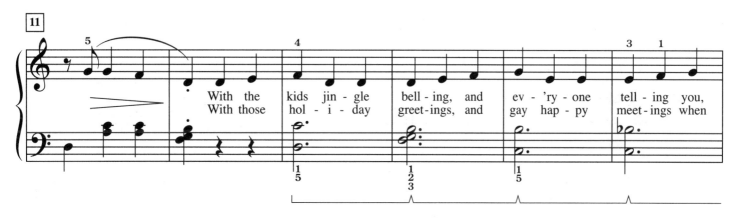

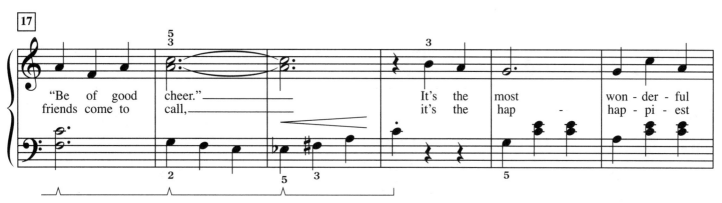

8

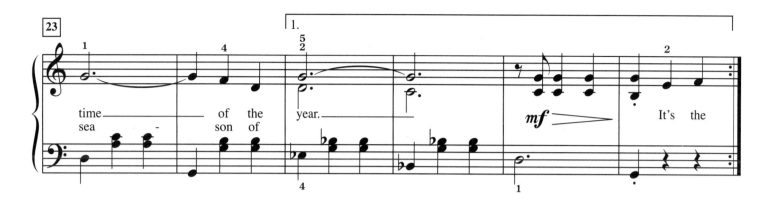

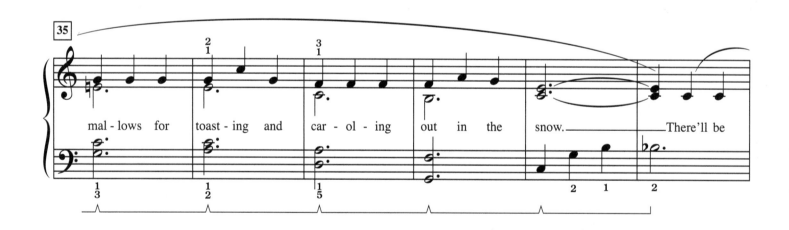

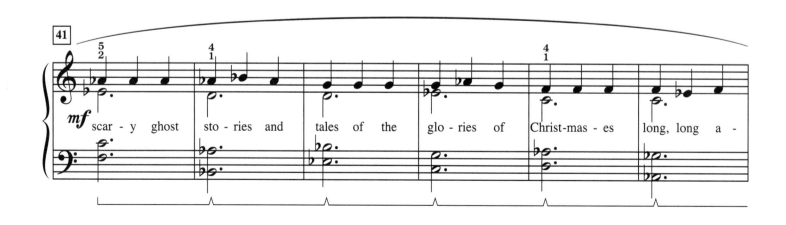

Let It Snow! Let It Snow! Let It Snow!

Words by
Sammy Cahn

Music by
Jule Styne
Arranged by Dan Coates

I'll Be Home for Christmas

Lyrics by
Kim Gannon

Music by
Walter Kent
Arranged by Dan Coates

Slowly, with expression

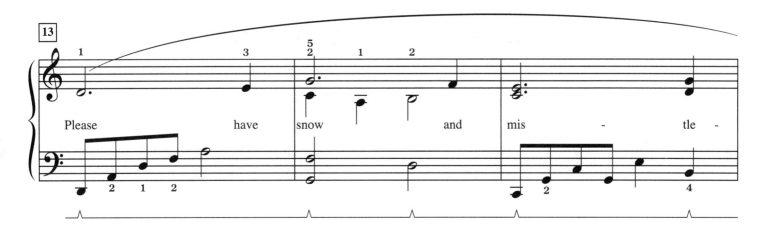

Please have snow and mis - tle -

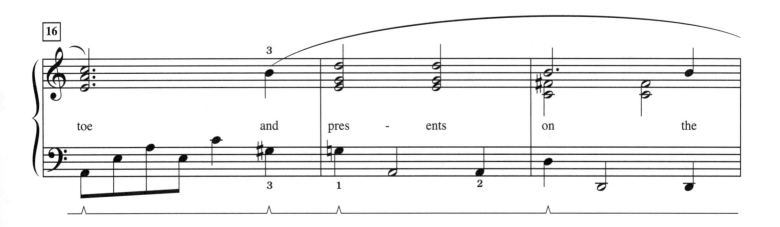

toe and pres - ents on the

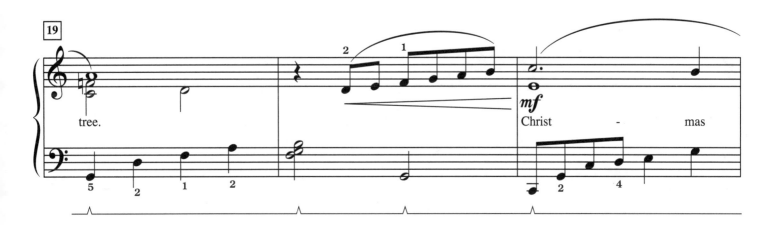

tree. Christ - mas

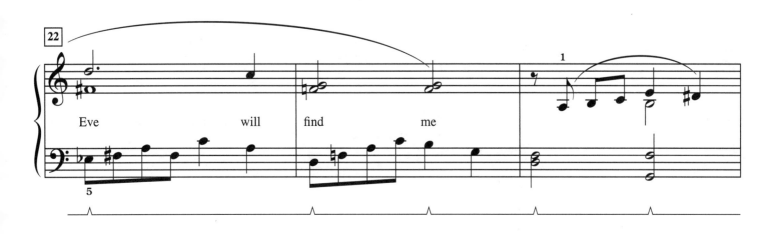

Eve will find me

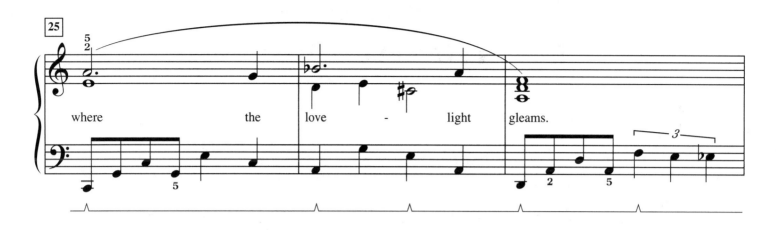

where   the   love - light   gleams.

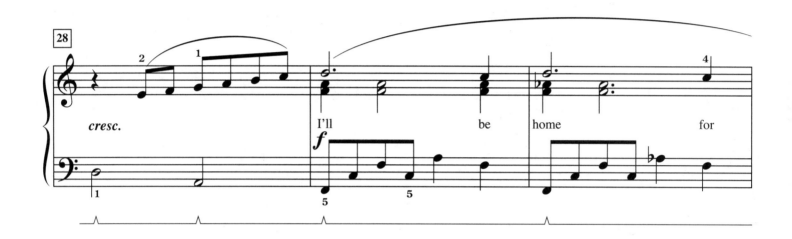

cresc.   I'll   be   home   for

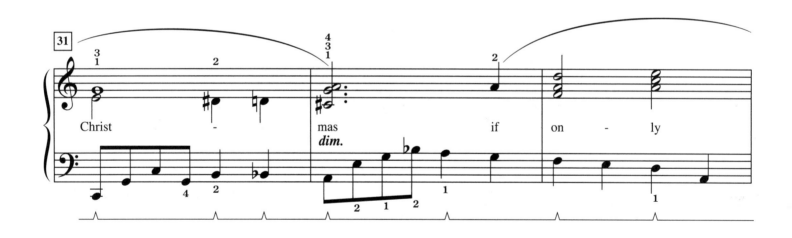

Christ - mas   if   on - ly

in   my   dreams.

There Is No Christmas
Like a Home Christmas

Words by
Carl Sigman

Music by
Mickey J. Addy
Arranged by Dan Coates

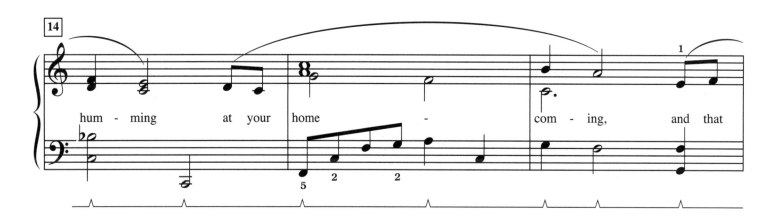

hum - ming   at your home -   com - ing,   and that

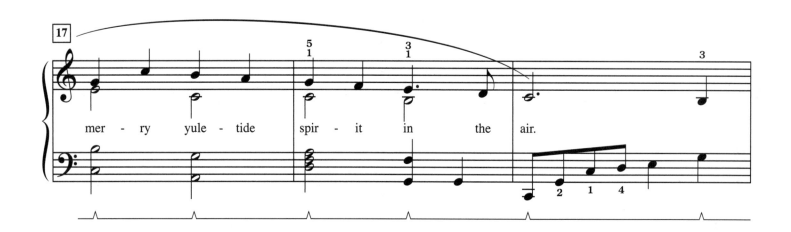

mer - ry   yule - tide   spir - it   in   the   air.

Christ - mas   bells,   Christ - mas   bells,

mf

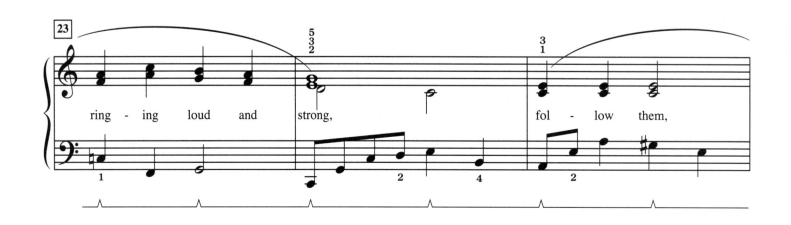

ring - ing loud and strong,   fol - low them,

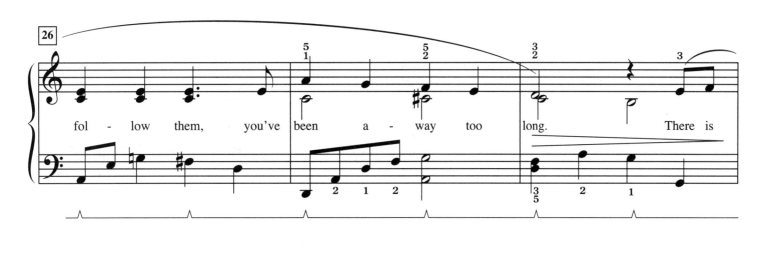

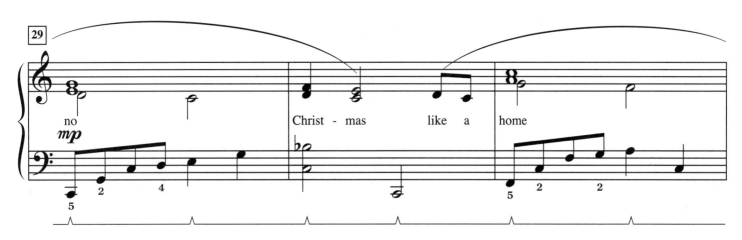

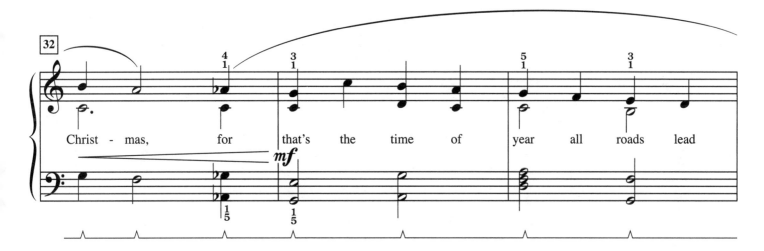

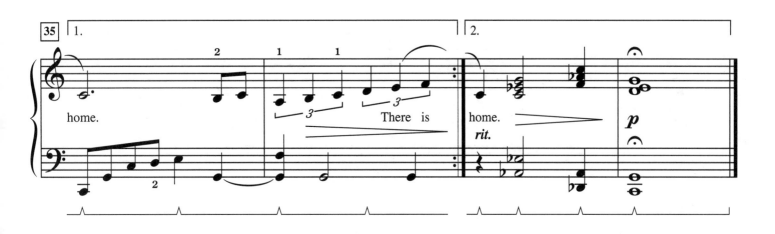

These Are the Special Times

Words and Music by
Diane Warren
Arranged by Dan Coates

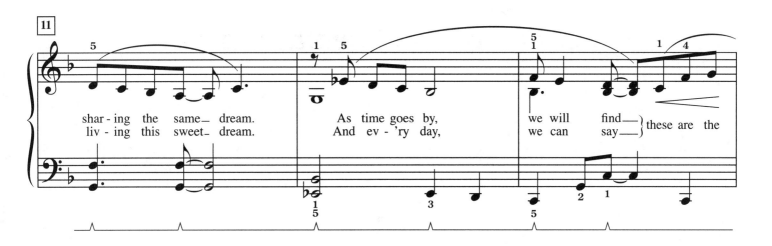

Sleigh Ride

Words by
Mitchell Parish

Music by
Leroy Anderson
Arranged by Dan Coates

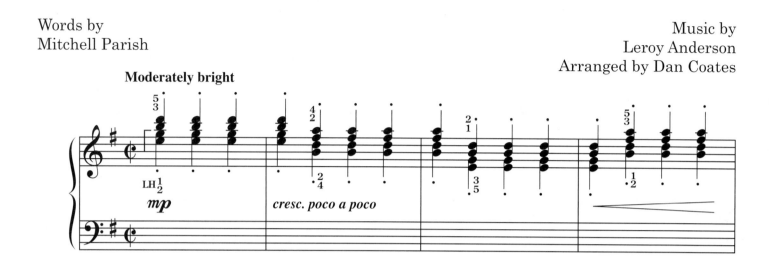

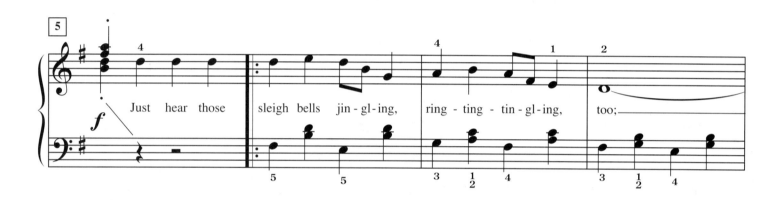

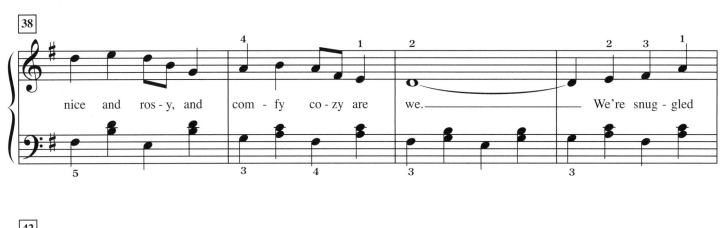

nice and ros-y, and com-fy co-zy are we._____ We're snug-gled

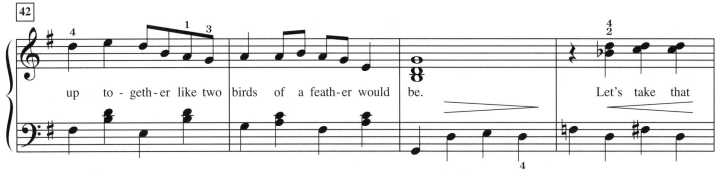

up to-geth-er like two birds of a feath-er would be._____ Let's take that

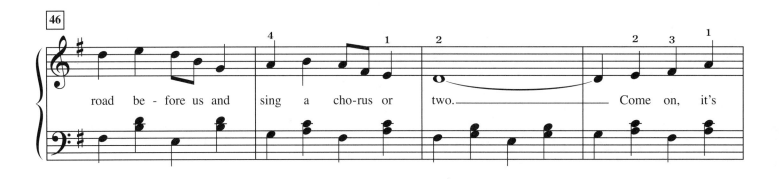

road be-fore us and sing a cho-rus or two._____ Come on, it's

love-ly weath-er for a sleigh ride to-geth-er with you._____ Just hear those

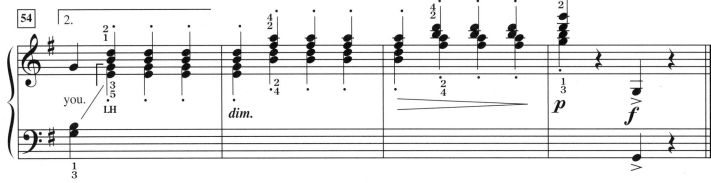

you.